JUST A THOUGHT

A collection of poems exploring the intricacies of the mind - including mental health issues, bereavement poetry, inspirational verse, and comical situations.

Mel Wardle Woodend

JUST A THOUGHT

First Printing: 2019

ISBN: 978-1-9999625-6-2 (DREAM WELL WRITING)

DREAM WELL WRITING

UNITED KINGDOM

www.dreamwellwriting.simplesite.com

A Dyslexia Friendly Publication

DEDICATION

This book is dedicated to my Mum Patricia Diane Wardle – for always nurturing and encouraging my creativity – and for ~~putting up with~~ listening to all my made-up stories and poems over the years!

CONTENTS

FOREWORD

Mel Woodend is an accomplished poet, having previously written several collections of thought-provoking work.

She will approach difficult subjects such as human frailties and self-doubt, but wrap them in a blanket of understanding and love.

I always feel cleansed reading Mel's poetry, for it makes you realise that life is full of light and shade, which she balances beautifully through her thought process and word play.

'Keep fighting for a better tomorrow.'

Nick Degg

ACKNOWLEDGEMENTS

Thanks are due to my husband Brent, for helping me to choose which poems to include in this collection, and being subjected to my many deliberations (mainly with myself but all out loud) in the process!

I would like to thank current Staffordshire Poet Laureate Emily Rose Galvin and performance poet Emma Purshouse for their back cover quotes, performance poet Nick Degg for his back cover quote and for the fabulous foreword, and thanks to John E. Smoke for the author photograph, and help with the art effects on the front cover photo.

Thanks also to you, the reader, for purchasing a copy of my book. I hope you enjoy the poems.

INTRODUCTION

This is my seventh published poetry book but the first in which I publicly acknowledge and address my mental health issues. For many years (twenty-eight precisely) I kept my struggles with Obsessive Compulsive Disorder, which I have had since I was nine, to myself as much as possible. I only really began to understand what all my 'worries' actually were, when I was in my early twenties, and I was twenty-five when I finally plucked up the courage to tell my boyfriend and parents who were immensely supportive and began to learn as much about the condition as they could so they could understand it, and me, a bit better and be able to support me.

I guess things came to a rather unpleasant head just before I turned thirty-seven. We had been through a lot of big life changes in a small space of time – including getting married, suddenly losing my Dad, starting two new jobs in the space of seven months, and moving house twice in ten months. Things got a bit much and I had the closest to a breakdown I have probably ever had, and realised I wasn't coping at all well with my O.C.D!

I went to the doctors, finally admitting I needed help, started medication, and started talking about having O.C.D.

For the first time since I was nine years old, I no longer felt embarrassed or ashamed and I realised I wouldn't keep it a secret if I had a physical illness such as a broken leg or the 'flu, so why should I treat my O.C.D. any differently?

Equally importantly, I wrote and performed a poem about it. This kick started me into addressing mental health issues in my poetry, and now, almost two years later, I am delighted to finally be publishing *Just a Thought* which I hope will help other people struggling with any sort of mental health issue to feel less isolated – and to know that acknowledging their thoughts and not feeling ashamed or embarrassed is such an important step....

PART 1 – OBSERVATIONS

A New Path

The end of something
Sometimes signifies the beginning,
Of a better life.
A bigger freedom,
A braver step,
On an unknown path.

Solitude
Is better than loneliness.
Judging oneself,
Knowing one's mind,
Understanding oneself,
On a chosen path.

Insomnia

Wide awake waiting for daylight as

The night crawls by.

Each minute an eternity;

Everlasting and endless

As I lie awake.

Sore eyes

Stare at the ceiling

Until

A thin shaft of light leaks through tired curtains as the foggy day dawns.

Morning peers blearily in at me through

The faceless window and my sleep deprived eyes

Resign themselves to another day of caffeine stimulants.

My dizzy legs stagger with exhaustion

And I feel sick,

Slightly unhinged,

Seemingly unattached from my body, my head disconnects and I am shaky and light.

I float through the day like an apparition;

I'm not really present.

It is too much to take in,

Too much to stay awake...

Insomnia is replaced by narcolepsy.

March

An in-between month that is not quite still winter,

But not yet spring.

Non-descript skeletons of fragile leaves hang brown and withered from hedgerows

Signalling the presence of a deadening winter passing through its life cycle.

Shrivelled and decaying like rotting corpses they hang soullessly

And in fields, lines of former sunflowers stand;

Heads hanging limply.

Dull. No colour.

Rows upon rows of emaciated bodies that once glowed brightly

With colour and life breathed from the summer sun.

Occasional daffodils bob in the breeze nodding a friendly 'good morning.'

A round faced crocus has fought its way up

Through solid earth and the beginnings of green grass to burst into the light and seize the day.

It contentedly unfurls petals and basks in the brief but

lengthening daily sunshine.
Cats can occasionally be seen sitting in a sheltered sunny spot outside
But most still slumber slit eyed on a cosy fireside rug.
The nubs of buds appear daringly on spiky twigs,
Brightening the grey bark with their promises of spring.
Grazes of green or pink tipped promises cannot be ignored or denied:
Hints of a fragrant summer to come...

The barren winter seems slowly to be packed away –
Banished in a box until another December arrives with frosty mornings.
Emerald greens of grasses will soon thrive,
And insects
On their brief but busy journeys
Will adorn bushes and trees.
But today,
Non-descript skeletons of fragile leaves
Still hang brown and withered from hedgerows
Signalling the presence of a deadening winter passing through.

Spillage of My Mind

As we tip towards ground

And the aeroplane falls,

My hand grips resolutely on my pen.

And I am trying to write out,

Trying to write through the pain,

Spilling the contents of my mind.

My mind, engulfed in you.

The Hour of Werewolves, Witches and Birdsong

Oh, brain!

Oh, body clock!

Why are you awake at such an unsociable hour?

Too tired to make a poem but too awake to sleep....

The night hours of werewolves, witches and vampires are still upon us,

Yet I can also hear a dawn chorus

Of birdsong.

Uncertainty

How do we know if the earth is round or flat?

Will we fall off backwards as all the seas pour out?

Will we reach a precarious edge and drop off falling forwards through space?

How do we erase our doubts?

How do we know if yellow is yellow and green is green?

Who decided that Monday to Friday is a working week?

How do we know the spellings of all the words we have learnt?

And the answers to what we seek?

How do we know we feel happy or sad?

Did someone teach us what it means to feel glad?

How do we know that all our feelings are true?

And we're not simply just quietly mad?

Who decided that we must wear clothes?

That at sixteen you can marry but you cannot drink, drive or vote?

Who decides how much money is worth?

And where do all the fallen autumn leaves go?

And when we die, do we even know we are dead?

Do we watch over loved ones left behind?

Are our souls up in heaven or is death a brick wall; a blank dead end?

How could we ever define?

All we really have is a certain uncertainty?

An endless list of questions with answers we will never know.

Life is ever shifting, and questions come and go,

As sure as the sun will shine, the moon will glow, the rain will fall, and the wind will blow.

PART 2 – THE STRUGGLE

Anxiety

You make my palms sweat –
And my hands start to shake.
I am imprisoned –
Needing to escape....

You flood my mind with worry –
Like slimy, insipid pea – soup.
I can't focus, cannot concentrate –
Blind panic stuck on loop....

You make my breathing shallow –
It comes in small, sharp gasps.
I need to get out of here –
And I need to do it fast....

You take control of my mind and limbs –
Like a robot I must obey.
As I leave my seat and run out of here –
Aghast and in dismay....

Broken

It was the hottest summer I had ever known.

Lawns lay dead across the U.K.

Bald, sallow grass,

Yellow like a jaundiced patient; frail and ill.

It was the summer that C.D.s took over the world

When Robson and Jerome spent seven weeks at the U.K. Number One,

Technology got cheaper

And we became; a throwaway society.

No one needed T.V.s repairing anymore –

And your work became scarce.

People bought into the cheap convenience

Of immediately buying a new T.V. or V.C.R. if their's broke.

But this made you broke and

Being broke

Irreparably

Broke you.

You tried to think positively – 'summer's always quiet' you'd say.

Everyone's outside

Enjoying the sun;

Not stuck indoors with the T.V. on.

But as seasons changed,

The dark nights came and

You realised this was not just a passing phase.

No work, no cash flow, and long, dark days and the darkness burnt a hole in you.

The winter ice lined the windowsill

And instant pasta framed our existence;

Squatting in a flat

Flatly unable to pay the rent; with only a gas fire to warm us.

In our living room, recirculated cigarette smoke

And the smell of Ariel

Hung in the air.

A seasonal sensory nasal mix as wet washing hung by the fire.

The air grew staler day by day

As '70s films flickered on T.V.

'Are we going to be ok?' I wondered as I was driven through the Christmas light display

By well-meaning friends trying to cheer my day.

I watched the white snow fall;

Clear and crisp contrasting with our grey.

And I knew...

You were not ok.

Just before I turned sixteen our existence fell apart

You were taken to hospital... and I was alone facing the dark.

I visited you and stronger and stronger you became day by day.

For my birthday you bought me a silver rollerball.

I still write.

Consumer Nation

We consume too much T.V.

Facebook fake news blurs reality.

We consume too much convenience food: burgers, chips and pop;

Full of additives and carbs. Our taste buds crave a junk food fix and we just can't stop.

We are the enablers consuming narcissistic behaviour from friends,

Whose draining self-obsession seems to be the latest trend.

We consume too much self-hate;

Size zero celebs, Snapchat, and Facebook 'likes' lure us in like bait.

We don't consume enough love for ourselves.

Don't be ashamed to say if you're struggling; if you need to ask for help.

We don't consume enough quality time with our best mates...

A night of laughter and catching up with friends can't be overrated.

We don't consume enough healthy, home cooked food.

Vitamins, fresh veg and a balanced diet can really lift the mood.

We don't consume enough music or poetry...

Food for the soul.

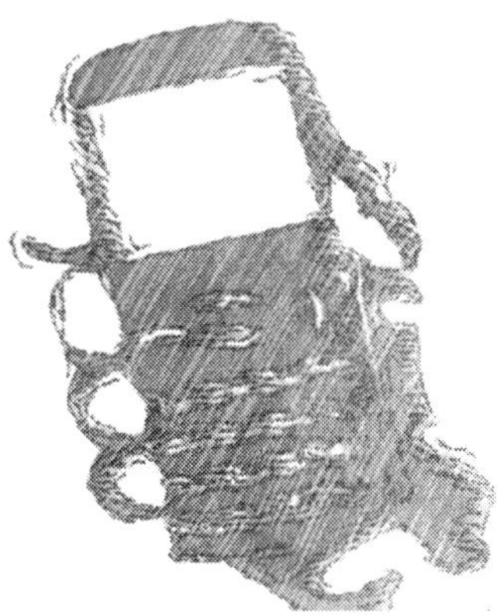

Conversation with My O.C.D.

CONFRONTATION AND RESPONSE

Me:

I am powerless as you freeze me to the spot.
I think I must be a 'bad' person to think the kind of terrifying thoughts that whizz in and out of my head as a 'what if?' and some days I can barely breathe.
I want - oh how I want to remove my head - not to die, you see but to swap my head for one that doesn't have this dodgem car circuit of your thoughts: banging and crashing and scraping and colliding.

I need to switch off sometimes and
I wish there was an electrical switch to flick you 'off' inside my head but knowing me it would probably be 'on / off / on / off / on / off / on / off.'
I can laugh about it sometimes but at other times I cry and sometimes I want to scream and kick the shit out of the door, the wall, myself...

I can't remember a day when I didn't have an intrusive thought from you, or a 'worry' or 'routines' that I had to do.
Not to protect myself. Never to protect myself. But to get others safely through the day.
I try to protect people. I mostly have 'responsibility O.C.D.' and I know, I KNOW, I'm an intelligent person and it seems crazy, ludicrous, insane... I know!

But I have to try because the alternative is unbearable.

O.C.D:

I am gleeful!
I think my wicked thoughts and I rub my hands together delightedly because....
I want to make you suffer.

I need you to feed me, to give me my power and
I wish I could stay in your head forever.
I am cruel, heartless, soul sucking, and cold.

I weave my magical thoughts inside your head - insidiously like

smoke curling from a fire.
I can get you to waste your life checking and checking and checking and checking, and worrying and worrying - oh the endless worrying!
I control you and I try with all my callous might to make you suffer.

The power resides in me.

Me:

My fists clench and unclench and my teeth grit to the point of chipping.
How have I wasted so many hours of my time, of my life, on you? You – a pathetic no one - a weasily little cheat trying to trick me with your lies and deceit.
I want to shove you right off the edge of a cliff. Yeah, I really do! And one day I might, I will... But not yet.

I need to believe in me.
Believe that I am not a bad person and I know I'm not really but sometimes it's hard to believe it....

I wish my brain chemistry was different but it's not and I do know there are far worse things in life to deal with than you.

I can see you now for what you are, for what you always have been:
A worthless time waster worming your way into my mind, infiltrating my brain and laughing at me every day as you watch me do my ridiculous rituals.
I cannot stand the idea of wasting any more years on you - wasting more of my precious time on your lies, your nasty threats, your taunts and your tantrums...

So I will try to ignore just a little bit more of you every day.

Conversational Implicature

I do not want to converse with a multitude of strangers.
People talk at me.
Not to me – they do not talk to listen back with mutual interest
But talk at me – invading my ears and my privacy.
The personal space inside my head.
I must rest and recuperate and think only thoughts that take me far far away.
Polite conversation is not for me
So do not draw me into your friendly chatter.
Do not drown me in incessant conversation.
My barriers are up. Please respect my privacy.
My ideas. My need to withdraw into myself.
Hat pulled down,
Sunglasses on,
Hunched amongst my papers
I seem abrasive, unfriendly...
It is not intentional.
I just don't have room for your incessant chatter in the confines of my head.
I need to think, to slowly turn the pages of my mind, as I unwind.
I am a closed book.

Daily Change

I want to change so I feel alive - not swamped by fear and negativity - so my day can just feel 'better,'

Not worry I'm touching someone's spit where they've licked the envelope and I'm opening a letter.

I don't want to think someone might die

When I touch my face, my nose, my eye...

And have to rush to wash my hands.

I want to feel safe – not sinking on quicksand – in my mind.

I want to go to bed and not have to stress

While I'm getting undressed –

Folding clothes the way my O.C.D. dictates and demands.

I would like to fold them only once - the way I choose - and still feel calm...

Or leave them chucked on the floor in a heap

But still be able to relax and go to sleep.

I want to simply get dressed

Without putting my leg in / out, in / out, in / out, in / out of my jeans like a mad woman possessed.

I want to get off the settee to go for a wee

And feel safety!

Simply standing and leaving the room would be divine.

A dream for me instead of having to touch the chair back every time.

I want to not have to discreetly do this in public every time I stand up too...

But to be free – just like you.

I'd love to just stand and walk across the room - any way, anyhow, anywhere,

Without ritualistically touching the back of my chair – because I'm afraid if I don't someone might die.

I have to protect my man, my mum, my pets, my friends

And the rituals seem to never end.

I avoid stairs – if I go up only once it might trigger something bad to happen – and if I go up twice

I'm afraid someone will die.

I am afraid and I want to live with freedom from my brain

Not live with the fear and compulsions I must repeat again, again, again, again.

The drugs do work to a certain degree

But there's still so much responsibility resting on me – to keep my loved ones safe:

I would like to make a change but to still feel safe: To be able to trust, believe, and know that they will be safe too,

Without my input, my mind, my O.C.D. telling me what to do...

Telling me it is all down to me,

It's a suffocating, devastating responsibility.

If I don't do it, they will die?

But the responsibility is killing me – stunting my enjoyment of life.

I find it hard to relax, enjoy, find positivity

As lurking on every corner is a – what if?

But - what if my brain could be rewired so I did not have these thoughts and fears?

It's an impossible ideal – it's been with me for thirty years.

I would like to believe that I can one day feel safe – find relief, reprieve...

But let's wait and see – before I let myself believe.

Firelight

I need calm, not mayhem;
My own inner peace - not your external conflict.
I need security, not instability;
A strong mind to reassure mine - not a weak one.
Attempts to undermine me stem from your own insecurity,
Scattering seeds of self-doubt into my mind
Like ash from a cigarette...
Greying me.

I need my own voice;
Not a devil on my shoulder,
Not a crooked voice blackening my soul,
Or a forked tongue dripping acidic poison into my ear.
I need my own version of truth;
Not your heavily adapted, edited, and over-dramatised version of events.
I need my wits about me;
Wise to your trickery, manipulation, and your arrogantly self - perceived dominance.
I need solid ground on which to stand;

To remind myself I am real
And I am here;
When your actions render me invisible.
I need to find my technicolour again,
Against the monochrome of your interference.

Now I can see through the transparency of your actions,
My only colour is red.
The colour of my indignance;
A volcanic explosion waiting to erupt.
Boiling anger burns through me,
My blood pumps once more and I,
I remember I am alive!
A furnace of flames sweeps through me
And I dance in the firelight.

Gyroscope Mind

My head feels full,

My mind distorts reality.

I am blind,

I can only see

Fear and fright and scary shadows in the night

As my mind plays tricks on me;

Convinces me I am mad or bad

With such convincing cruelty.

I have said I would like to replace my head

With one less complex, more free,

But without my own head, my irrational fears

I really wouldn't be me.

So I wend my way on life's tumultuous path;

This gyroscope for my mind.

It turns and twists every which way it wants,

I'm just dragged along for the ride.

Sometimes my fears are poisonous, fierce,

Raised like a rattlesnake ready to bite.

Some days I defy them, quash them down

And they slither silently into the night.

My gyroscope mind lurches and reels.

Sometimes I'm unsure which way is up

But I know to my demons I will never give in, never give them the satisfaction.

I will conquer and quell and still my fears, and I will always never give up.

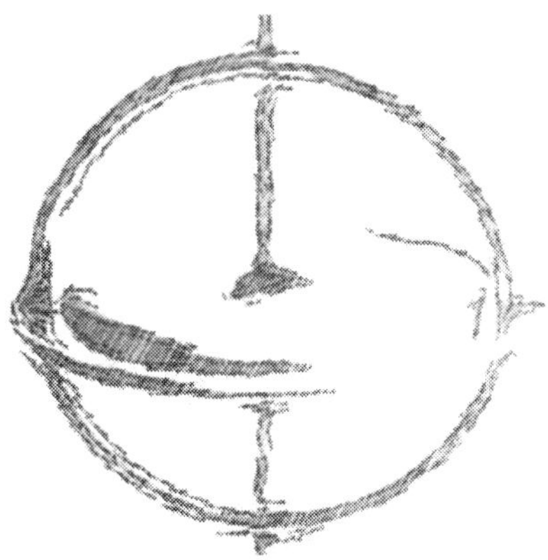

Hollow Laughter

Hollow laughter
And eyes that lack sparkle; even on the sunniest autumn day
When warm golden light reflects and refracts through the
hazel of my eyes.
Nodding and smiling agreeably and making plans
Gets me through another day.
It's my armour you see? My outer shell.
The only part of me that I let you see, while
I ache - inside.
Doubled over, I stop, stand still to steady myself as the pit of
my stomach pulses – a physical pain
Now the summer has gone....

Gone for another year; the warmth that penetrated my body,
my brain, my core...

Tenderly warming and allowing my tense and aching muscles to relax - a brief reprieve as the summer light let days linger late into the evenings.

Only now the dark evenings have returned

And I hear the dread in your voice again - echoed now in my own subconscious.

Nodding and smiling agreeably I steel myself.

My armour looks strong and impenetrable.

Check my eyes if you really want to know.

How Can I Write?

How can I write anymore?

How can I put pen to weary paper -

Its sinews staring blankly back at me.

My head is devoid, full of otherness-

Tucked in by the blanket of life

Squeezing

Smothering.

How can I write?

On a busy street where chaos surrounds me

And danger lurks on every street corner

Where I concentrate as if my life depends on it

Crossing streets, dodging bullets disguised as four wheels with noxious gases and drivers in control.

How can I write?

Amid the turmoil.

People

Pushing

Swarming

Frantic.

Antlike.

Shouting into hands-free technology,
Dragging screaming children by the hand.
The noise incessantly screams at me.
Where is the peace?
The peace to silence my mind.

Then I am there where
The ocean laps like a kitten
On the shore.
Soft, innocent,
Warm...
I drink in this view.
My mind stills.

How can I write?
When my head is so full of beauty and trauma
And love and loss
And life is a whirlpool of possibility and maybe and yes and no
and what if?
How can I write?

O.C.D.

Don't worry - be happy....

So easy to say but not easy to do when

facing an eternal ongoing war raging inside your mind against

O.C.D.....

We all have our quirks - our routines - our orders - getting up, getting ready, morning routines, and leaving for work....

But O.C.D. creates an ongoing cycle of angst - I must check the door four times, I must check the door four times, I must check the door four times, I must check the door four times....

What if I've left the hair straighteners on?

What if they cause a fire?

What if the flat burns down - the cat dies and I – I cause all this to happen?

What if?

So in this endless tortured cycle I must check and check and check again - until it feels just right.

My anxiety builds - other compulsions creep in - I get distracted - anxiously turning on and off the light.

Then finally. I am ready to leave. I step out the door with a

final glance back, lock the door – I definitely did turn the key
But just to be sure I check the handle again and again - there
must be no uncertainty!

Then heart racing, palms sweating, a trickle of sweat on my neck, I hurriedly walk away....
My breathing calms, cools, steadies. I've got past this stumbling block....
Now pick up the pace, I'm late, having to race - to work.
My boss simply won't understand.... What can I say? What excuse can I conjure up today?

Anything but the truth for fear of judgement - of laughter - of rejection – of being shunned by the 'normal' people - the cool people - the people that don't admit to having any worries that haunt them night and day.
But in this denial to others I deny myself too.
I trap myself into lies, into a forced fake smile, forced to fit in, to pretend and....
That's just not me.

So here is the truth! I have O.C.D.
It used to control me when I hid, alone and afraid of being me – but why shouldn't I be me?

You see? Now I can admit it is part of me

I am free.

It is no longer controlling me –

It's a deflated balloon falteringly fluttering around the room

Losing power then falling down -

Defeated to the ground.

It is lifeless, whereas I am living - free....

And yes, I still have O.C.D.

And yes, it is a daily battle of questioning wars inside my head,

But now I don't care what people think, I am not afraid to be me instead.

Judgemental idiots can walk away

And those who stay are the ones who matter

Who will always be there, who care

About me.

And in allowing myself not to care; to shrug off the way past people have judged,

I am not judging myself,

I am just being me,

So I am free.

Park Bench Paradise

Park bench paradise,

Sleeping outside.

Reddened, painful fingers fumble with thin sleeping bag zip,

You've nowhere to hide.

No door to close.

Outside you survive on adrenaline,

Nowhere is really safe.

Keeping your wits about you,

Hunker down, close your eyes, feel your heart race.

No door to close.

Some nights below freezing

Your heart barely beats at all,

It slows, almost giving up –

Mind and body succumb to the cold.

Hypothermia, pneumonia,

Frostbite, a transgression:

No job, no money, no money, no deposit, no deposit, no home –

You're stuck in this endlessly oppressive recession.

No door to close.

A mismatched shanty town

Of brightly coloured tents,

This isn't the third world poverty of India, Nairobi or Mexico City...

It's 'affluent England's' Milton Keynes, seaside town of Falmouth, and Tunbridge Wells in Kent.

Thin fabric buffeted and blown; your shivering figure sits and waits

Cross legged in the icy, biting wind

While a few feet away, rosy faced shoppers burst busily into a coffee shop

To buy their customary coffee and cake within.

A row of brightly coloured tents

Line a cold, grey, concrete underpass.

Their colourful cheeriness belies

Your bleak and empty eyes inside.

No door to close.

Mercury plummets into minus figures,

Yet you're all still stuck out here – the old, the young, the weak, the strong, the frail;

No one is exempt

From the risk of being derailed

From this rollercoaster ride of life - one minute you're sitting safely at the top

Where you've found life's luxuries: A home, a family, a job.

But just one slip, one bad turn of the dice, you can fall and lose it all.

Kicked out, jobless, homeless; on the streets like a stray, downtrodden dog.

So, who is helping

To counteract your plight?

Who is helping you

Find a bed for the night?

A rise in unaffordable housing and benefit sanctions,

Work contracts for zero hours.

Employment is almost impossible

With no address – you are frozen – you've lost all power.

No door to close.

Soup kitchen volunteers

Dole out food and steaming hot tea;

Bringing cheer and warmth,

Sharing their own time generously.

But… your fight is getting harder;

Because people like you, who sleep on the streets

Are the ones we can see.

We know you've got no home, no bed, no warmth, and not enough to eat.

No door to close.

But what about the hidden homeless?

Sofa surfers; relying on their mates for help....

Or night after night sleeping in a car

Just to get a tiny bit of shelter?

If you're really lucky you might land yourself a job!

Then your benefits will stop. Because surely you won't need them when you're earning a 'living wage?'

Then, the old struggle resumes....

You've got money to eat but not enough to get a deposit to get off the streets and into your own place!

No door to close.

You are working –

But for what? For who?

Lines drawn tight on your taut face;

The stress, the desperation of your situation starts to show through.

No door to close.

And slowly your resolve dissolves

As your life

Falls down

Around you.

So, what will you do?

How can you live your life?

With no door to close

In this park bench paradise?

Physical

Pain twists the sinews of your mind,
Turns your heart inside out,
Makes you physically sick and stops you getting out of bed.
Your legs fail,
Your mind fails,
Your soul fails,
You fall.
You cannot rouse yourself.
'Mind over matter' they say...
But nothing matters when your mind is broken.

September Squalls

Most days are doable, now,

Yet some days the air still stifles me.

Choking on my own breath my heart aches heavily

Knowing you are not here.

A simple phone call that cannot be made is my reminder.

A small shock every time I forget - for a second - then remember.

Most days are manageable, now,

Yet still there are some when a storm

Unpredictably rages out of nowhere – its squalls sharply slap my face;

Knocking me off balance, briefly.

I stumble, then steady myself.

Head down I push against the raging wind; until calm comes and I can lift my head and breathe once more.

Sticking Plaster Heart

Broken pieces of a jigsaw heart,
Slowly stuck back together piece by piece after being pulled apart....
By love, by loss, by life,
But I will fight and strive to survive.

Piece by piece and patch by patch
My sticking plaster heart is etched
With memories happy, sad, bitter, glad,
Loved, lonely, treasured, terrible, alive, afraid, carefree....

Like a patchwork map
Revealing rocky routes travelled,
Roads walked,
And circuits sprinted lap by lap.

My sticking plaster heart marks the passing of time -
Sometimes so full of love it might explode,
Sometimes empty
Like a moonlit road....

Always ready to give and love
Ever ready to shut down, close up, withdraw....
Like a castle drawbridge, its portcullis will close.
Cutting off as self-preservation grows.

My sticking plaster heart pours with the blood of a thousand
knives stabbing straight into my heart.
Cut off the blood flow. Sharp. Shock. Think. Stop. Start....
Lie quietly still, until
I feel a gentle rhythm start again; a soft gentle beat...

Hear it beating louder. Stronger...
Only I have the power, to patch up my sticking plaster heart,
Piece by piece.
Only I have the power, to teach myself to heal.

Street Corner Kid

He's a street corner kid leaving school with nothing to show for the blazer the uniform,

Nothing to show apart from a report that says he 'wouldn't conform.'

He congregates on street corners with mates in labels they can't really afford;

Unwashed, unkempt, and unemployed.

Standing together, they dress the same: An understated statement

Firming friendships as solid as cement.

Looking for fun found in their new freedom

Away from the mindless misery and mortification.

Every day a struggle at school:

He could not read so he was ridiculed.

Acted up, he played the fool,

You see, he'd do anything for acceptance, to look cool.

He'd do anything to detract,

To take the focus off the fact....

'I can't do it, Miss.'

Anything but that.

But cool status is slipping; out here the real world is hard.

There's no money to withdraw; the cashpoint's swallowed his bank card.

He browses the Job Centre but each advert says you need at least three G.C.S.E.s

And minimum grades of A to C.

The apprenticeships look good but how can he apply when he can't fill in the application form?

Couldn't they see It wasn't that he 'wouldn't conform,' he just couldn't conform?

Day by day, his trendy teen status starts to slip into disarray....

A cider can clutched in nicotine stained hand and a couple of spliffs get him through the day.

Choose 'life?' But how? When he can only just exist?

Hundredth failed job search result – he might as well just get pissed.

No job, no education, just an allowance from the state

That barely pays the rent, the food, the bills, the rates....

Mates slowly slip away.

Off to work or uni. Now he's facing each longer, lonelier day;

He is purely existing.

He is not really living.

Existing on money borrowed for pick-ups scored from dealers

in the park…

Existing only for his next hit now, that will surely get him through the dark.

What used to be hip, fun; a social trend

When hanging out with friends

Has become a slow descent down into misery

He's locked in a despairing downward downfall with no way to break free.

Now injecting filth into live giving veins,

The irony is not lost but his addiction numbs the pain.

The pain of poverty - of purely existing -

Of not being able to embrace his life – he is not really living.

Until one day there sits a man slumped, veins pumped,

In the stairwell of the high-rise block – his worldly possessions in a bag next to him, dumped.

People stare and use the other door...

They step carefully around him on the floor...

Unwashed unkempt unemployable - in a heroin induced haze,

His eyes are glazed.

The Irony

The irony these days is that obesity is on the rise,

Convenience food is cheap and people generalise –

Making fun if you're overweight,

Sneering: 'Who ate all the pies?'

But the reality is that to 'eat fresh'

Costs a bomb unless

You manage to get to the reduced section in time to browse and take your time

Looking for the bargains that are best.

But in this hamster wheel rat race, we are all short of two necessities:

The old adage is true; time really is 'money'

And have we really got time

To go home and cook fresh from a recipe?

So if you're not slaving away, working to make ends meet,

You're slaving at the stove asleep on your feet...

Trying your best

To make something nutritious to eat.

Society judges if you cave into a fast food burger diet

But whizzing through the drive thru for a 99p burger and only a few p extra for fries

Is cheap

And the convenience cannot be denied!

It's so much cheaper than buying fresh,

Even though you know that fresh is best,

When you're tired and skint and just haven't got time

To slice and dice and all the rest.

But ironically cheap processed foods are unhealthy

And will ultimately give you less energy.

So if you could only summon the energy up, to shop the reduced section, cook and freeze in bulk,

You'd soon be saving pennies.

But with prices rising in living costs I don't see your earnings increasing to match,

So you work the extra hours to try to make ends meet – grab a burger – and dash...

A quick, cheap food fix.

And you risk the health and energy crash....

The Mask

'I'm fine thank you' she brightly says

When exchanging the time of day.

With lipstick on, a jaunty step and a smile,

No one can tell what turmoil is inside

Her mind; chaotically wired, arcing, sparking, with connections working loose.

If only insulation tape was insular, it would be the sticking plaster she would use

To hold it together as she steps outside - head high - day by day into the world.

She soldiers on until back home by night she safely curls

Like a foetus - a vulnerable baby – her tears flow, she loses control, and unstoppably sobbing she shakes.

She has fought with her mind as gallant as David with Goliath, Perseus with Medusa, and Gellert with the Wolf - and now her body aches.

Falling into a restless sleep,

Her mind now enters the place where nightmare dreams reach...

A ghostly white woman - haggard, pallid and sunken eyed - exits her bed at first light,

Dresses in her bathroom, and puts on her lipstick; vivid and bright.

The Only Solid Thing is Concrete

Life and death:

A faltering first step on

Baby legs.

Innocent, wobbling, unsteady.

Later - youthful impatience:

Impetuousness

Stepping forward towards adulthood.

Promises, prospects, the future.

Firm, steady steps:

A grounded reality.

Until

It gets too much.

A frailty:

Faltering steps.

One forward

Too many back....

Too many betrayals, bereavements, battles.

The one inside my head tells me to stop.

To let go.

Falteringly I climb.

I am ready.

I slip.

Fall down

And

D

o

w

n

And....

Bleak hard concrete rushes up to meet me:

Firm and assured.

Twenty-First Century Sensory Overload

Why is there so much noise?

So much noise everywhere?

The T.V. yelling at me,

The washing machine vibrating wildly; a spin crescendo like an orgasmic woman.

A tap drips

And someone speaks to me;

Trying in vain to be comprehended over all - this – noise.

I cannot listen.

I cannot hear; my mind shuts down to block the sounds out.

A bubble rises in me and I want to smash everything:

To hurl the T.V. remote through its flat glossy screen like an axe through flesh,

To wrench the neck of the tap out of its scrawny socket.

I need to dull the receptors in my brain

To tune out the raw frenetic screeching

As the metal drum discordantly batters and penetrates my mind.

I want to cover my ears and drown out the sound of the human voice speaking...

But I do none of these.

Instead, I nod through gritted teeth.

Eyes vacant, I stare into space.

Outwardly my face is expressionless, as my mind shrivels in turmoil.

PART 3 – INSPIRE

Clarity

The turmoil of the sea
Clears my mind,
Like waves washing over sand disturbed by the footprints and actions of others.

The confusion created by footprints running this way and that...
Scuffed up, kicked up, messed up, roughed up,
Pushed together and pulled apart.

The sand particles are the thoughts careering around my mind;
Blown this way and that by the icy biting bitter winter wind.
The collision of rational thought with emotion.

But the sea is cool and calming.
Its powerful presence like a strong hand on my shoulder
Wraps its arms around me: protecting, reassuring, enfolding me in its strength and surety.

Beckoning me forward until I see only water - water and horizon.
No people, no buildings, no man- made chaos.
Just the power of the moon and tides; the pull of the ocean

Hypnotic over me as I stand;
Cold water lapping against my legs,
Swaying slightly with its rhythmical roll.

The sea is not still, yet it stills my mind.
It's strength and surety, power and purity
Calm and quell my turbulent thoughts - bringing inner peace to turmoil.

Tranquility.
And I am balanced once more
By the clarity of the sea.

Colour

Nuances of colour

Splash through my mind,

Occasionally relieving

The black and white.

New Day

The dawn awakens

As a gentle reminder

To embrace the day.

Nurture

For

My love

To find you,

Just open your heart;

I will nurture your soul

And hold my heart against yours

Like clear and fragile glass.

Please keep it safe,

For I break

So easily

Too.

Own Path

I'm on my own path.

Don't ask me to follow you;

I'm not in the herd.

Pixilate

A patch of light shifts behind the thick darkness of the curtain.
The room is still engulfed in black and
My eyes won't adjust easily to the dark.
Without glasses on to strengthen my vision I can only see pixilated shadows.

Yawning, I reach for my glasses from the wooden dresser and position them on my face.
Getting out of the snug warmth of bed is an effort I can barely make.
But yawning,
I do.

At the window, pulling at the curtain I reveal a magical light outside.
The sky is a thousand hues turning from black to blue;
More beautifully colourful than a purpling bruise.
Stripes of black and grey cloud layers slash through the shifting shades.

As nature wildly splashes streaks of ink across the sky
It paints a glorious golden sunrise into the scene –
Separating jet-black tree lines from the still dark, waking forest.
A spectrum of dark aubergine to sparkling magenta shades
now fill the sky.

The sun's golden light radiates heat,
Expectancy,
And life,
As animals and human life rises in a simultaneous dawn chorus
to start the day.

Searching

What is perfection?

We will always be
Searching
For that perfect wave, the perfect ride, the perfect break, the perfect words, that perfect somebody.

But what if there is no such thing as perfect?
I am not perfect
And neither are you.
Even heroes have flaws!

The world has many doors
That close cruelly on you;
Shattering expectations, hopes, dreams,
Reality; when you least expect it.

It is how you react, how you counteract, that can create perfection in an imperfect world.
Rise up, try, cry if you need to in anger, despair, frustration, and sorrow.

But never let go, keep holding on, don't lose your grip,
Keep fighting for a better tomorrow.

And while you're hanging on, teeth gritted through the duck dive or the bumpy ride,
You might find hiding in the shadows where you least expect it to reside -
A gradual glowing jewel
Of perfect imperfection deep inside.

Drawn out by friendship, warm support, a push, encouragement,
And you will surprise yourself when you finally understand what true friends mean
When they jump up on chairs and declare:
'You've always had the power.... You just had to learn it for yourself....'

But deep down you know you will always want, and you will always need, that 'Little bit of help' from true friends because 'No man is an island entire of itself...'
And true friends who give you that power, that push, that little bit of self-belief - to begin to believe in yourself...

True friends who help you to find the gradual glowing jewel hidden deep within...

True friends are a jewel to be treasured and nurtured forever too.

We will always be

Searching

For that perfect wave, the perfect ride, the perfect break, the perfect words, that perfect somebody.

But when we finally look deep inside,

That's when we will know;

As long as we have fun in the surf, enjoy the ride, have a laugh along the way,

Grasp our opportunities and try to be kind with our words every day,

When we look around

We might realise we have found

That the world is not so bleak and grey,

If we treasure the perfect imperfection in ourselves and our true friends who we have found along the way....

What If?

What if I'm in love?
What if I'm in love with something so dangerous, and passionate, and scary, and fierce and real....
That the feelings fizz out of me, frighteningly powerful, like a firework ready to explode?

What if I'm in love?
What if I'm in love with something that has the power to sweep me off my feet, to knock me senseless, to enliven me and to crush me all in such quick succession
That it leaves me reeling; unsure of which way is up or how to put one foot in front of the other to continue on my wobbly path?

What if I'm in love?
What if I'm in love with something so heady, and overpoweringly scented, that the scents overwhelm my senses like sweet flowers on a burning, hot summer's day....
Filling my heart with the feeling, belief and idea that anything is possible, potentially?

What if I'm in love?
What if I'm in love with something as unpredictable as the sea that it leaves me soaring atop the crest of a wave one minute; queen of the world
Then diving straight down into the pit, stomach lurching as I fall and spin, out of control as the wave wipes me out; to splutter and surface and try again?

What if I'm in love?
What if I am in love with life itself?

Words

Life is too short
To leave the important words unsaid....

Words like
'I'm sorry' and
'I love you.'
Words that mean so much.

Words can shape or break a heart.
Choose carefully because the damage cannot be undone.
Forgiven – always.
Forgotten – never.

So lay the foundations of love and say what you mean.
Have the uncomfortable conversation – red faced and toe squirming if you have to.
But have it. Embrace it. Experience it. Feel it.
Honesty can never be regretted.

Life is too short
To leave the important words unsaid.

ABOUT THE AUTHOR

This is Mel's seventh published poetry collection. Her other books include four poetry books aimed at an adult audience – spanning themes from synaesthesia, nature, and bereavement, to humour, holidays, and love. Her other two poetry books are for children. Both children's books are dyslexia friendly, as is her full-length children's story book, also published.

Mel has edited volumes of work for other poets and novelists, as well as compiling, editing, and publishing two poetry anthologies for an environmental arts organisation. She has produced various anthologies for charity, collaborated on publications with other artists, and is regularly commissioned to write poetry.

Mel's own poetry has been published to date in a variety of U.K. anthologies, and her non-fiction work has been published internationally in both print and online magazine publications.

Although somewhat more land locked than she would like, Mel visits the sea as regularly as she can, where she enjoys bodyboarding and avoiding jellyfish. When at home, she spends time with her family; including her pet cat and guinea pig, who find themselves the subject of many a poem.

Mel works full-time as a writer; writing, editing, publishing, facilitating poetry and creative writing workshops, and organising spoken word events including a regular monthly poetry slam. She loves performing poetry at slams and open mic events, and is looking forward to performing for the first time at festivals this summer. Mel holds an MA in Creative Writing, a Postgraduate Certificate in Professional Studies in Education - Difficulties in Literacy Development, a Postgraduate Certificate in Children's Literature, and is a member of the National Association of Writers in Education.

If you would like to receive notifications of Mel's forthcoming events and publications, please sign up to her website newsletter free of charge at

www.melwoodendwriting.com

She can be found additionally on Facebook, Instagram, and Twitter:

facebook.com/melwardlewoodend/

instagram.com/melwardlewoodendauthorandpoet/

twitter.com/wardlewoodend

If you have been affected by any of the issues addressed in this book, some helpful websites offering mental health support are:

www.mind.org.uk/

www.ocdaction.org.uk/

www.ocduk.org/

PREVIOUS PUBLICATIONS

Poetry Collections

A Poet's Poems (2015)

Journeys and Memories (2015)

Poems of Spring (2016)

Natural Colours (2017)

Children's Poetry Collections

What Am I? An Alphabet of Animal Poems (2017)

I Smell Fish and Chips and Worms Too (2017)

Children's Fiction

Tails of a Little Brown Mouse (2018)

Charity Poetry Anthologies

There Is No Planet B – Act Now (2018)

The Friendship Collection – Children's Collection (2018)

The Friendship Collection – Poetry (2018)

The Friendship Collection – Short Stories and Young Adult Fiction (2018)

Global Warning (2019)

FORTHCOMING PUBLICATIONS

Novella

My Diary of a Cat Owner – coming soon....

22819688R00059

Printed in Great Britain
by Amazon